Peter F. Copeland

CIVIL WAR UNIFORMS

Coloring Book

Dover Publications, Inc.

New York

To Sadi Koylan, an old confederate

INTRODUCTION

At the time of the Civil War, many nations, including the United States and the Confederate States, attempted to clothe their troops in uniforms emulating those of the army of Napoleon III of France, then thought to be the finest in Europe. At the beginning of the war in 1861, the small U.S. Army was reinforced by many militia units clothed in exotic, sometimes rather antique uniforms in many different colors and styles. While newly appointed Confederate officials tried to raise a volunteer army to defend their borders, the Southern states also sent into the field colorfully clad militia regiments. As a consequence, in early battles the newly raised Southern and Northern armies contained companies and regiments in a wild variety of styles of dress. Scottish Highland-style units, in bonnets and kilts, served alongside regiments clothed in the colorful dress of the Algerian Zouaves. Lancers and dragoons were seen in steel helmets and breastplates. Soldiers outfitted in the green dress of the Italian Bersagliere sharpshooters fought Southern soldiers dressed in gold epaulettes, shakos and pipe-clayed crossbelts. Some Confederate companies wore fringed rifle dress reminiscent of the American Revolution of nearly a century before.

In those early days of the war, many of the newly raised regiments of both sides took the field in scarcely any uniform at all, wearing civilian dress of stovepipe hats and claw-hammer coats, armed with antique flintlock muskets and pistols, huge Bowie knives, shotguns and homemade pikes. Some regiments had companies which were each uniformed differently. This created an odd appearance on the parade field and many problems in the field of battle. At the first battle of Bull Run, on July 21, 1861, some Southerners in blue fought Northern soldiers clad in gray uniforms. Needless to say, this caused great confusion.

As the war progressed, most of these exotic costumes were abandoned and both sides took on a more standard dress. Soldiers of the Union forces adopted a sensible dress of caps (or slouch hats), dark blue fatigue jackets, and light blue trousers. Southern soldiers appeared in gray (or, as often, in butternut-brown) jackets, trousers and slouch hats. Gone also were the motley collections of weapons and accoutrements which had equipped the early volunteers. Northern manufacture supplied the Union troops; battlefield capture and European military materiel run through the Union naval blockade of Southern ports armed and equipped the Confederate forces.

Throughout the war soldiers of the U.S. Army generally appeared in dress and with equipment more or less as specified in regulations. This was not the case in the South, where regulation dress was seldom obtainable by the armies in the field.

Published in Canada by General Publishing Company, Ltd., 30 Lesmill Road, Don Mills, Toronto, Ontario. Published in the United Kingdom by Constable and Company, Ltd., 10 Orange Street, London WC2H 7EG.

Civil War Uniforms Coloring Book is a new work, first published by Dover Publications, Inc., in 1977.

International Standard Book Number: 0-486-23535-1

Manufactured in the United States of America
Dover Publications, Inc.
180 Varick Street
New York, N.Y. 10014

1. Private, Company D, 19th Illinois Volunteers, the Ellsworth Zouave Cadets, U.S. Army, 1861. The 19th Illinois was the first of the gaudy Zouave units to be raised in the U.S. In the spring of 1861 Company D was named after an early war hero, Colonel Elmer Ellsworth. The private wears a dark blue jacket with red cuffs trimmed with yellow, and with brass buttons. His cap is red with a dark blue band. His trousers and the sash about his waist are bright red. His leggings are brown and his shoes and waist belt are of black leather. A headquarters tent is in the background.

2. Private, 1st Florida Cavalry, C.S. Army, 1861. This was one of the many Confederate units which were unable to supply regular cavalry equipment to its men at the outset of the war. The troopers of the 1st Florida regiment were originally armed with shotguns in place of carbines and sabers. This Florida horseman lacks boots and spurs. He has procured a Southern-made Cofer revolver which he has stuck in his belt because he has no proper holster. His cap is blue, his jacket gray with yellow corporal's stripes, shoulder stripes and buttons. His canteen is painted red, its strap and his waist belt are brown. His trousers are dark blue and his shoes are of black leather.

3. Private, 39th New York Volunteers, the "Garibaldi Guard," U.S. Army, 1861. This unit, raised in May, 1861, was composed mainly of foreigners. It included one Italian company, one French, three Hungarian, three German, one Spanish and one Swiss. The private's uniform is the green color of the Italian Bersagliere sharpshooters. His black hat, with green feathers and brass letters on its front, is also patterned after them. His collar, cuffs and the edging on his coat are red, as is the stripe on his trousers. His leather equipment, gaiters, haversack and shoes are black and his canteen is gray. His knapsack is black; a red blanket is rolled and secured to the top. His buttons are brass.

4. Drummer boy, 8th Regiment, New York National Guard, U.S. Army, 1861. The uniform this drummer boy wears was in the style of those of the Mexican War. He wore it to the front in 1861 and throughout the war. His cap is gray with a dark blue band and a small brass device on the front. His collar is dark blue with black braid and brass buttons. His jacket is gray with dark blue shoulder straps. His trousers are white and his shoes are of black leather. His drum has a tan head; its shell is dark blue with red and white hoops and white cords. His drumsticks are of brown wood and the trumpet is brass with white cords. The carrying strap of the drum is of white leather, as is his waist belt, which has a brass plate.

5. Virginia Militia Volunteer, C.S. Army, 1861. Southern militia units uniformed their men as best they could, some being ornately outfitted, others only partially equipped and clothed. This volunteer wears a Corsican cap of dark blue with a red stripe and tassel. His jacket is of coarse gray cloth with dark blue trim. His trousers are of butternut yellow-brown homespun. His shoulder belts are brown, and his waist belt is black with a brass buckle. His buttons are brass, and his checked shirt is red. He carries a Virginia manufactury musket of 1806, converted from flintlock to percussion. As did many volunteers of '61, in his belt he carries a Bowie knife with a wooden handle and brass trim. His shoes are of brown leather. The lady's dress is green with white collar and cuffs.

6. Private, 5th New York Zouaves, U.S. Army, 1861. Commanded by Colonel Abram Duryee, this regiment is reported to have been one of the finest units to serve in the Union Army. The private wears the colorful dress uniform of the regiment. The turban on his head is white with a dark blue tassel. His jacket and shirt are dark blue with red trim. The cummerbund, or sash, about his waist is dark blue with light blue edging. His trousers are red and his gaiters are white. His shoes are of black leather as are his waist belt, cap box and cartridge box. His buckle is brass. The canteen at his side is gray; its strap is of brown leather. A sutler's tent (the 19th-century equivalent of the modern PX) is in the background.

7. **First Lieutenant, Company A, 5th Georgia Volunteer Infantry Regiment, "The Clinch Rifles," C.S. Army, 1861.** All of the companies of this regiment wore different uniforms, a frequent occurrence early in the war. The regiment lost over half its men at the battle of Chickamauga in 1863. The lieutenant wears a dark blue coat and cap, or kepi, and light blue trousers. His cap device is white, as is his trouser stripe and the edging on his collar and cuffs. His buttons, the belt plate and the trim on his sword and scabbard are of brass. His sash is red and his shoulder straps are light blue with white bars and gold edging. His shoes, sword scabbard and waist belt are of black leather.

8. Captain, 1st Rhode Island Volunteer Infantry Regiment, U.S. Army, 1861. First commanded by Ambrose Burnside, this regiment served at the first battle of Bull Run. The uniform was of Burnside's design. This captain wears a "Burnside Blouse" of dark blue with brass buttons. His trousers are light blue and his canteen is gray with a brown leather strap. His waist belt, cap box, shoes and sword scabbard are of black leather. His gauntlets are buff; his cap is dark blue with a brass hunting horn (the infantry device) on the front. His belt plate and sword and scabbard trim are of brass. His shoulder straps are sky blue with white bars and gold edging. In the background is a soldier's grave at Fair Oaks, Virginia.

9. Private, Company C, 20th Mississippi Infantry Regiment, C.S. Army, 1861. This soldier has been issued an old-style flintlock musket. Such antique weapons were frequently discarded early in a battle, usually to be replaced by a percussion-type gun captured during combat. He wears a black felt hat, cocked up in 18th-century fashion, with a tin star on the front. His gray coat has black cuffs and collar and brass buttons. His canteen is of white metal. The haversack at his side is of white duck linen, as is its strap. His trousers are of homespun butternut brown. In his belt he has thrust a pistol. His waist belt, cap box and shoes are of black leather. The small Southern town has a recruiting office and a Confederate flag made according to its first pattern, the "stars and bars."

PLANTER'S HOTEL

VOLUNTEERS WANTED!

10. Private, 2nd New Hampshire Volunteer Infantry, U.S. Army, 1861. This regiment was one of the early Federal units clothed in gray, and an old-fashioned uniform with a tailcoat reminiscent of the early 19th century. The 2nd New Hampshire served at the first battle of Bull Run, and in every major engagement of the Army of the Potomac throughout the war. The private wears a gray cap with a red band. His gray coat is trimmed with red at the collar and cuffs. His buttons and belt plates are brass and his belts and shoes are of black leather. His trousers are gray with a red stripe. His haversack and strap are black. His cap devices are brass. Behind him another member of the regiment wears a winter overcoat of sky-blue kersey.

11. **Private, 6th Pennsylvania Cavalry Regiment, "Rush's Lancers," U.S. Army, 1861.** The only regiment of lancers to serve with the Union Army, the 6th Pennsylvania was considered to be one of the finest cavalry regiments to serve with the Federal forces. The lance was abandoned in 1863 and the regiment thereafter served as ordinary cavalry, armed with carbines, pistols and sabers. The private wears a dark blue cap with brass insignia. His jacket is dark blue with brass buttons and shoulder scales. Edgings on jacket and braid on the collar are yellow. Belts and boots are of black leather, and his trousers are dark blue (later changed to light blue). His saber has a brass hilt and steel scabbard. His lance is of ash with a steel point and a red banner. His spurs are brass, as is the oval plate on his shoulder belt. Behind the lancer we see a 20-pounder Parrott rifled cannon.

12. Second Lieutenant, C.S. Marine Corps, 1861. The Confederate Marine Corps numbered only about 1000 men. It served in naval stations on the Southern coast, aboard vessels of the Confederate Navy, and took part in some of the land battles of the war. Little is known about the uniforms and equipment of these sea soldiers. Officers seem to have worn a variety of uniforms. Our lieutenant wears a gray coat, in the style of an officer of the C.S. Navy, but with gold army-style insignia of rank on collar and cuffs. His buttons, watch chain and sword and scabbard fittings are of brass. His cap, also in the style of a naval officer, is gray. His coat is edged in black, and his scabbard and shoes are of black leather. His trousers may be either gray, dark blue, or white. His vest is gray. In the background is the first Confederate man-of-war, the *Lady Davis*.

13. Sergeant, Company B, 4th Texas Volunteer Infantry Regiment, C.S. Army, 1861. Commanded originally by Colonel John Bell Hood, the 4th Texas served the Army of Northern Virginia as part of the famed Hood's Texas Brigade. This sergeant wears a black slouch hat with a tin star at the front. His jacket and trousers are gray, trimmed with black edging, and his sergeant's stripes are black. His buttons are brass and his sergeant's sash is red. His shoes and belts are of black leather. His hickory shirt is red.

14. James H. Lane as a volunteer of the Kansas Militia, U.S. Army, 1866. Lane, a former Lieutenant Governor of Indiana and a fierce abolitionist, eventually became head of Kansas irregulars in the Federal service. They participated in the bloody border warfare between Kansas and Missouri, where no quarter was given or asked. Lane wears civilian dress of the day with military accoutrements, a common outfit among early volunteers of both sides. He wears a black beaver hat, dark blue coat, white shirt and black tie. His waist belt and shoes are of black leather. His trousers are gray and on his breast he wears a red-white-and-blue ribbon—a Union cockade. His musket sling is white, and his belt plate and sword hilt are of brass. His bayonet has a steel blade and a brass hilt. In the background is an unlimbered 12-pound howitzer and its caisson.

15. Private, Company F, 4th North Carolina Infantry Regiment, "The Rough and Ready Guards," C.S. Army, 1861. The organizer and first captain of this company of North Carolina mountaineers was Zebulon B. Vance, later Governor of the state. After the war, he described himself as having been "awfully rough, but scarcely every ready." The company fought at Antietam, Chancellorsville and Gettysburg, among other bloody actions. This private wears a black hat with the company device in gold letters on a pale blue background. His jacket is gray with dark blue trim. His buttons and belt are brass. His belts, shoes and bayonet scabbard are of black leather. His trousers are butternut brown.

16. Private, City Guards Company of Arkansas, C.S. Army, 1861. The uniform of this young volunteer from Arkansas is both neat and sensible. His cap is dark blue with a white band. His coat is gray with white collar and cuffs. His buttons are brass, as is his Confederate belt plate. His belts are white and his cartridge box and shoes are of black leather. His trousers are dark blue, and his musket sling is white.

17. Private, 4th Michigan Infantry Regiment, U.S. Army, 1862. This young soldier from the West wears a dark blue kepi and fatigue jacket, dark blue trousers, and brown gaiters, or leggings. His belts and shoes are of black leather, as is his musket sling. The blanket atop his pack is gray, and his buttons and belt plate are brass. An officer's tent stands behind him.

18. Lieutenant, Alabama Cavalry, C.S. Army, 1862. This officer from an Alabama cavalry regiment wears a light brown slouch hat with a red feather in it. His coat is gray and nonregulation single-breasted. His buttons and belt plate are brass and his sleeve and collar braid are yellow. White corduroy trousers are tucked into brown leather cavalry boots. His belt and cap box are black leather and his sash is red. His sword has a brass hilt and a white metal scabbard.

19. First Sergeant, 3rd New Jersey Cavalry Regiment, U.S. Army, 1862. Also known as the First United States Hussars, this regiment adopted a uniform similar to the Hussar regiments of the armies of Europe. The sergeant wears a dark blue pillbox cap edged with yellow and with a brass plate on the front. His dark blue dolman-style jacket is trimmed with yellow braid and edgings. The buttons and belt plate are brass. His trousers are light blue with a yellow stripe. His belts are of black leather, as are his shoes. His sword scabbard is of white metal. His rank stripes are yellow. An army mail wagon stands in the background.

20. First Lieutenant, Hampton's Legion of South Carolina, C.S. Army, 1862. Organized, equipped and commanded by Wade Hampton, a wealthy South Carolina planter, the legion contained four companies of cavalry, six companies of infantry, and a battery of artillery. They fought at the first battle of Bull Run under Hampton's command. The lieutenant wears a brown slouch hat with a red feather in it, and a brass palmetto device on the front. His jacket is gray with yellow collar, cuffs and trim. His trousers are light blue and his belt, pistol holsters and boots are of black leather. His belt plate, buttons, spurs and sword hilt are brass. His gloves, which he holds in his right hand, are buff. His sword has a steel scabbard. Behind him is a company commander's tent with the blue and white palmetto flag of South Carolina flying over it.

23. Captain, C.S.S. *Old Dominion*, **C.S. Navy, 1862.** Officers of the Confederate Navy had a prescribed uniform, consisting of a steel-gray double-breasted frock coat and trousers, a naval cap and shoulder straps like those of the U.S. Navy. The uniform of the captain bears little resemblance to the regulation uniform. He wears a short cavalry-style gray jacket with dark blue cuffs and vest. His trousers are gray. His belts, sword scabbard and shoes are of black leather, as are his pistol holster and binocular case at his side. His shirt is white; his tie black. His buttons, buckles and scabbard trim are brass. In the background is a 10-inch Rodman naval gun.

24. Private, 43rd Battalion Virginia Cavalry, C.S. Army, 1862. This unit, the famed Mosby's Partisan Rangers, led by the "Gray Ghost," John Mosby, harassed the rear areas and flanks of the Army of the Potomac. The private wears a black hat, gray jacket with yellow trim and brass buttons and belt plate. His vest is green and he wears across it a gold watch chain. His trousers are gray and his boots and pistol holster are of brown leather. His buttons, sword hilt and scabbard fittings are of brass, as are his spurs. In the background, before a line of soldiers' tents, flies the Confederate battle flag.

21. Captain, U.S. Marine Corps, 1862.
The Union Marine Corps of the Civil
War was a small organization which,
like its Confederate counterpart, pro-
vided personnel for war ships afloat,
and guards for naval stations ashore.
Marines also served with the Union
armies upon occasion. The captain is in
full dress uniform. His cap is dark blue
with a brass device on the front and a
yellow pompom on the top. His coat is
dark blue with yellow patches on the
collar and cuffs. His waist belt and
sword straps are of white leather. His
cap box, sword scabbard and shoes are
of black leather. His trousers are white
and his sash red. His buttons, sword
fittings and belt plate are of brass; his
epaulettes are gold.

22. Corporal, 3rd Company Richmond Howitzers, Army of Northern Virginia, C.S. Army, 1862. The unit was originally the artillery company attached to the 1st Virginia Regiment. Soon after they became a separate artillery battery. The corporal wears a gray cap with a red band and a brass letter on the front. His jacket and trousers are gray; his corporal's stripes and the stripe down the sides of his trousers are red. His sword is brass, the scabbard is of black leather with brass fittings. His belt, holster and boots are of black leather. Buttons and belt plate are brass. His shirt is white and his tie is black.

25. Corporal, 20th Maine Infantry Regiment, U.S. Army, 1862. This soldier wears the field service uniforms with full field equipment adopted by the Army of the Potomac early in the war. His fatigue jacket is dark blue with brass buttons. His trousers are dark blue (a peculiarity of this regiment; most Union soldiers wore light blue trousers). The haversack at his side is black, as is its carrying strap. His belts and shoes are of black leather. His canteen and tin cup are gray. His knapsack is black with a gray blanket rolled and secured at the top. His kepi is dark blue with a brass device on the top. His musket has a black leather sling.

26. Private, 14th Tennessee Infantry Regiment, C.S. Army, 1862. The regiment, which served in 1862 in Western Virginia, was originally armed with old flintlock weapons. This private provides an excellent example of the typical Confederate foot soldier in marching order. He traveled lighter than did his Yankee counterpart, usually wrapping most of his belongings in a blanket roll slung over his shoulder. He wears a brown slouch hat, gray jacket and trousers. His buttons are brass. His canteen has a grayish-brown cover. His black haversack is worn at his side behind his blanket, which might be green or brown. His belts are of white duck linen. His cap pouch and bayonet scabbard are of black leather, as are his shoes.

27. Lieutenant, Company G, 1st United States Sharpshooters, U.S. Army, 1862. Carrying on the great tradition of riflemen in America's wars, the 1st and 2nd Regiments of U.S. Sharpshooters served mainly as snipers, armed with Sharps rifles and specially-made sniper's rifles with telescopic sights. The men of Company G came from Wisconsin. Our Lieutenant wears a uniform entirely of rifle green. His sash is red. His belts are of black leather, as are his shoes. His belt plate is of brass as are the buttons on his coat and the device on top of his cap. He is armed with a sniper's rifle and a Colt pistol. Because he is a rifle officer, he does not carry a sword.

28. Private, Maryland Guard Zouaves, C.S. Army, 1862. Originally part of the 47th Virginia Infantry Regiment, the Maryland Zouaves eventually became part of Steuart's Brigade of the Army of Northern Virginia. The private wears a red kepi with dark blue band. His jacket is dark blue trimmed in red with brass buttons. His trousers are dark blue with a red stripe; the gaiters are white. His canteen has a brown-gray cover and brown leather strap. His bayonet scabbard, cartridge box and shoes are of black leather. The hilt of his bayonet is of brass.

29. Captain, Washington Artillery Battalion of New Orleans, C.S. Army, 1862.
Composed originally of wealthy men of New Orleans, this unit dated back to
1838. It served in the Mexican War and in every battle with the Army of
Northern Virginia throughout the Civil War. This Louisiana captain wears the
uniform of his battalion, another Confederate unit that wore Union blue. His
cap is red with a dark blue band and yellow trim and insignia. His frock coat is
dark blue with yellow metal buttons and sleeve braid. His shoulder straps are
red with white bars and gold edging. His sash is red and his trousers light blue
with red and yellow stripes. The leather of his shoes and waist belt is black;
that of his binocular case and strap is brown. His sword has a brass hilt and
scabbard trimming. The scabbard itself is of black leather. The English 12-
pounder is limbered—attached to the two-wheeled vehicle on the left.

30. Private, Louisiana Tiger Zouaves, C.S. Army, 1862. Organized by the adventurer Roberdeau Wheat, this unit was recruited mainly among the Irish stevedores along the New Orleans waterfront. After the death of their commander at the battle of Gaines' Mill, Virginia, the Tigers never again functioned as an effective unit. The private wears a straw hat with white hatband. His shirt is red with brown trim, and his Zouave jacket is brown with red trim. His buttons and belt plates are brass. His trousers are of mattress ticking striped blue, red and white. His leggings, or gaiters, are white. His shoes, cartridge box and belts are of black leather.

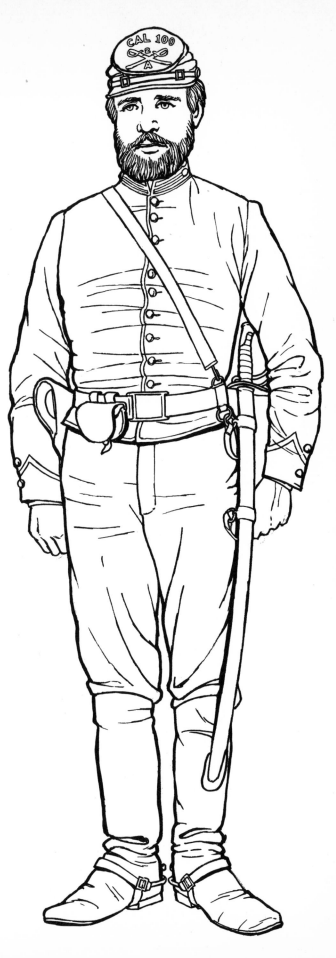

31. Private, Company A, 2nd Massachusetts Cavalry Regiment, "The California Hundred," U.S. Army, 1863. The men of Company A were California volunteers who came east to join the Union army. Organized in Boston in 1862 they were mustered into the 2nd Regiment and arrived at Yorktown, Virginia, in February, 1863. Our private is in the field dress of a Union cavalryman. His cap is dark blue with brass insignia. His dark blue jacket is edged and trimmed in cavalry yellow with brass buttons. His sword hilt and belt plate also are of brass. His trousers are light blue and his belts, cap box, holster and boots are of black leather. His saber has a white metal scabbard, his spurs are of **brass.**

32. Mule Driver, Army of the Potomac, U.S. Army, 1863. Runaway and liberated slaves served the Union armies in many capacities —as teamsters, laborers, cooks and, in some all-black regiments, as combat soldiers. This mule driver wears a brown slouch hat with red hatband. His undershirt is red and his vest is of green and white stripes. His jacket is of grayish-white cotton, and he wears army trousers of light blue. His cavalry boots are of black leather. His teamster's whip is brown. An army wagon is in the background.

33. Captain of Artillery, Provisional Army of the Confederate States, 1863. Uniforms prescribed for the Confederate armies by regulation were often far different from those worn by officers and men in the field. This artillery officer is in walking-out dress—a prescribed uniform. (In the field he might easily be seen wearing a slouch hat and a short jacket.) His cap is artillery red, with dark blue band and gold trim. The double-breasted frock coat is of cadet gray with red collar and cuffs, and edging. His vest is also gray. His buttons are brass and his insignia and sleeve braid are gold. His trousers are light blue with a red stripe. His shirt is white and his cravat, or tie, is black. His shoes are of black leather.

34. Quartermaster, U.S. Navy, 1863. Sailors and petty officers were issued white summer uniforms and blue winter uniforms of similar cut. Photographs of the time show many sailors wearing their dark winter jumpers with white summer trousers—presumably the uniform of the day on certain vessels at various times. The quartermaster wears a dark blue cap with a black band. His jumper is dark blue with white stripes at collar and cuff. His tie is black and his petty officer's badge on his left is white. His trousers are dark blue or white. He carries a brown telescope with brass trim. His shoes are of black leather.

35. Major, Medical Department, Army of Northern Virginia, C.S. Army, 1863. The Confederate Medical Department was originally organized to contain 1000 surgeons and 2000 assistant surgeons. Each regiment in the field was to have one surgeon, one assistant surgeon and one hospital steward attached to it. Surgeon's uniforms were to be the same as those of other officers, but with black facings. Our major wears a gray kepi with gold trim and a gold device ("MS" for Medical Service) on the front. His coat is cadet gray. His cuffs, collar and the edging on his coat are black. His trousers are light blue (though gray was often worn instead) with black stripes edged in gold down the sides. Medical officers adopted a green sash, like that worn by Union Army medical officers. His buttons and belt plate are brass, and his belt and shoes are of black leather. On the table are bottles of drugs and a chemist's mortar and pestle.

36. First Sergeant, The Irish Brigade, Army of the Potomac, U.S. Army, 1863. The Irish Brigade, originally composed of several New York regiments, was made up of Irishmen who, having been transported from Ireland for treason, had come to New York. The brigade fought in the battles of Fredericksburg and Antietam, among others. The sergeant wears a dark blue kepi topped with a red cloverleaf. His jacket is dark blue with green collar, cuffs and sergeant's stripes. His buttons, belt plates and sword hilt are of brass and his sergeant's sash is red. His canteen is gray with a brown leather strap. His belts, bayonet scabbard, and shoes are of black leather. His trousers are gray. An iron artillery mortar is in the background.

37. General Robert E. Lee, C.S. Army, 1863.
Lee, Commander of the Army of Northern
Virginia, is seen here in the uniform he
normally wore in the field—a variation of
the regulation general officer's prescribed
dress. He wears a gray felt hat with light
brown hatband, rather than the gold-laced
kepi. His double-breasted frock coat is cadet
gray, as are his trousers. (General officers
were supposed to wear dark blue trousers
with gold stripes at the sides.) As insignia
of rank General Lee wears simply three gold
stars on his collar rather than the regulation
three stars within a gold wreath. He does
not wear the prescribed sleeve braid or the
buff facings to his coat. His sash is the general officer's regulation buff, as are his
gauntlets. His belt is gold with a gold buckle.
The binocular case and strap are of brown
leather. His sword has a gold hilt and brass
scabbard fittings. His shoes and sword
scabbard are of black leather. His shirt is
white, his tie black and his vest is gray. His
buttons are brass.

38. Captain, Invalid Corps, U.S. Army, 1863. The corps, established in the spring of 1863, was composed of disabled officers and men who could still perform limited service such as guard and garrison duty. The captain wears a dark blue kepi, a light blue coat with dark blue collar and cuffs. His buttons, belt plate, sword hilt and scabbard fittings are of brass. His trousers are light blue with dark blue stripes at the sides. His sash is red and his shoulder straps are dark blue with white bars and gold edging. His belt and shoes are of black leather; his gauntlets are of buff leather.

39. Missouri Guerrilla, Quantrill's Border Raiders, C.S. Army, 1863. The pro-slavery Missourians and the abolitionist Kansans had been engaged in open warfare along the border for 10 years before the Civil War began. The fighting continued on a larger scale throughout the war years. William Clarke Quantrill led a band of pro-Confederate guerillas who raided, burned, and killed Union men along the Kansas-Missouri border during the war. Quantrill did not have a Confederate commission and his men were not regularly enrolled as a unit in any Confederate army. They wore mixed civilian and military dress, incorporating captured items of Union army quipment. The guerilla shown here wears a butternut-brown Confederate-style jacket with brass buttons. He has on a brown slouch hat and a red and white striped shirt. His vest, captured from the Yankees, is dark blue with brass buttons. He wears light blue Union army trousers and a captured waist belt of black leather with brass belt plate. His boots are of brown leather. In his belt he carries a pair of Southern-made Dance Brothers .36 caliber Texas pistols; in his hand he carries a captured U.S. Spenser cavalry carbine.

40. Private, 44th Indiana Volunteer Infantry Regiment, U.S. Army, 1863. This is the dress of the Union troops who served in the Federal armies of the West, where the war was a scene of almost continual movement, maneuver and counter maneuver. Soldiers involved were almost constantly on the march. Union troops in Tennessee, Georgia and Mississippi marched light, whenever possible, often carrying their few belongings wrapped in a light blanket roll, Confederate fashion. The private wears the black slouch hat popular with the Western soldiers. His dark blue fatigue jacket has brass buttons. His trousers are light blue and his belts are of black leather, as are his shoes and musket sling. His belt plates are brass, and his canteen has a brown-gray cover.

41. Lieutenant, U.S. Navy, 1864. A variation of the prescribed naval officer's summer-dress service uniform is worn by this lieutenant. He sports a civilian straw hat with a black band popular with officers serving with the navy in Southern waters. His dark blue sack coat (not officially authorized to be worn until January, 1865) has brass buttons and gold-lace insignia at the cuffs. His shoulder straps are dark blue with white bars and gold edging. His civilian checked shirt is red and white. His trousers are dark blue, or white, for summer wear. His shoes and sword scabbard are of black leather. His sword has a white grip and brass fittings, as does his scabbard.

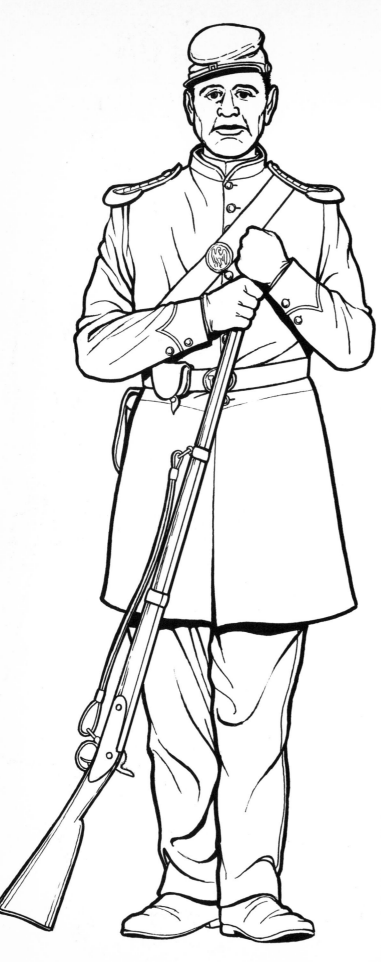

42. Private, 107th United States Coloured Troops, U.S. Army, 1864. During the course of the war over 300,000 blacks were enrolled in the U.S. Army in the infantry, cavalry, heavy artillery, field artillery and one engineer regiment. The private wears a modified dress uniform for guard duty. His kepi, coat and trouser stripe are dark blue; his trousers and the edging at his cuffs and collar are light blue, the color of the infantry. His musket sling, belts, cap box, cartridge box and shoes are of black leather.

43. Dr. Mary Walker, Medical Department, U.S. Army, 1865. Though most army nurses were men, some women on both sides served with distinction as nurses. Dr. Mary Walker tended wounded soldiers under fire on the field of battle with such bravery that she was awarded the Medal of Honor—the only woman who has been so honored. Dr. Walker is shown in a uniform of her own design. She wears a dark blue skirt, trousers and tunic with brass buttons. The gold medal and clasp has a light blue ribbon. Her cap is dark blue with a black ostrich feather.

44. Major General Ulysses S. Grant, Commander of the Army of the Potomac, U.S. Army, 1865. Grant wears a field variation of the regulation general officer's dress. He wears a black tie and felt hat; his shirt is white. His frock coat, dark blue with brass buttons, has black collar and cuffs. His shoulder straps are dark blue with white stars and gold edging. His vest and trousers are dark blue. He does not wear the authorized badge ("U.S." in silver, within a gold wreath) on his hat, the general officer's sash, a sword or sword belt. His shoes are of black leather.

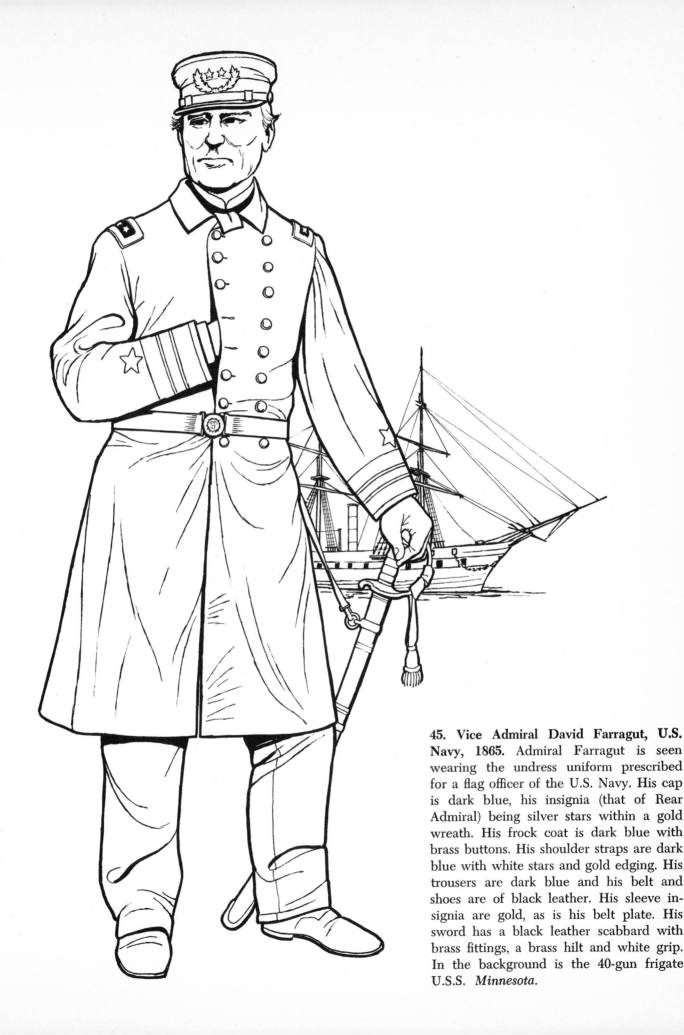

45. Vice Admiral David Farragut, U.S. Navy, 1865. Admiral Farragut is seen wearing the undress uniform prescribed for a flag officer of the U.S. Navy. His cap is dark blue, his insignia (that of Rear Admiral) being silver stars within a gold wreath. His frock coat is dark blue with brass buttons. His shoulder straps are dark blue with white stars and gold edging. His trousers are dark blue and his belt and shoes are of black leather. His sleeve insignia are gold, as is his belt plate. His sword has a black leather scabbard with brass fittings, a brass hilt and white grip. In the background is the 40-gun frigate U.S.S. *Minnesota*.